2 **THE LONGUES-SUR-MER B... STRONG POINT**

4 **THE ATLANTIC WALL**

Hitler's directives for the construction of the Wall — 4
The Wall, one of the *Reich's* prized propaganda tools — 7
The Todt Organisation — 10
Rommel and the Atlantic Wall — 12
The Atlantic Wall on the eve of the D-Day Landings — 14
A thousand bunkers from the Mont Saint-Michel to the Seine estuary — 15

16 **THE LONGUES-SUR-MER BATTERY**

Built in record time — 17
• *The four casemates* — 19
• *The battery command post* — 21
Intense attacks before D-Day — 22
• *Aerial bombing* — 22
• *Naval bombardments and German artillery retaliation* — 23
The surrender of the Longues garrison — 27
• *The Atlantic Wall, a futile fortification?* — 28
• *The Longues-sur-Mer battery after the German retreat* — 31

32 **DISCOVERY TRAIL**

Zone tertiaire de Nonant - 14400 BAYEUX
Tel.: 02 31 51 81 31 - Fax: 02 31 51 81 32
info@orepeditions.com - **www.orepeditions.com**

Editor: Grégory Pique
Editorial coordinator: Corine Desprez
English Translation: Heather Inglis
Graphic design: Éditions OREP - **Layout:** Sophie Youf

ISBN: 978-2-8151-0724-2 – © Éditions OREP 2023
All rights reserved – Legal deposit: 2006

THE LONGUES-SUR-MER BATTERY, AN ATLANTIC WALL STRONG POINT

The German coastal artillery battery at Longues-sur-Mer, located on the Calvados coastline, is an excellent example of an Atlantic Wall strong point. The Longues bunkers are far from unique and, today, the Normandy coastline still hosts the more or less preserved relics of thirty or so of the *Wehrmacht's* artillery batteries between the Mont Saint-Michel and Le Havre. The German battery at Longues is particularly noteworthy since it is the only one to have preserved its guns, after strangely escaping the fervent post-war scrap merchants.

Located in the heart of the allied assault zone, between the American and the British landing beaches close to Arromanches, the Longues battery is one of the highpoints of the D-day landing route. The site not only bears witness to the last great fortification built by man, but is also a tangible example of the German occupation in Normandy and a leading place of remembrance of World War II.

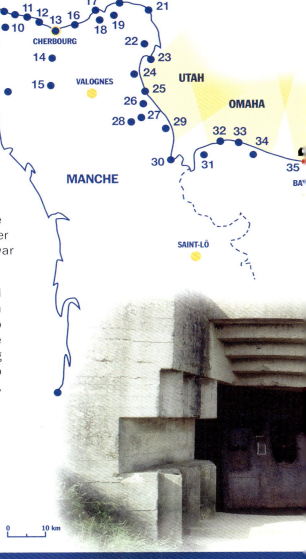

20.	Néville-sur-Mer
21.	Gatteville-le-Phare
22.	La Pernelle
23.	Saint-Vaast-la-Hougue
24.	Crasville
25.	Quinéville (Mont Coquerel)
26.	Saint-Marcouf (Crisbecq)
27.	Azeville
28.	Amfreville
29.	Saint-Martin-de-Varreville
30.	Bay of Veys
31.	Maisy
32.	Pointe du Hoc (Cricqueville-en-Bessin)
33.	Vierville-sur-Mer
34.	Colleville-sur-Mer
35.	**Longues-sur-Mer**
36.	Asnelles
37.	Ver-sur-Mer
38.	Douvres-la-Délivrande
39.	Colleville-Montgomery
40.	Ouistreham
41.	Caen
42.	Sallenelles
43.	Merville-Franceville
44.	Houlgate
45.	Auberville
46.	Bénerville (Mont Canisy)
47.	Trouville-sur-Mer
48.	Pennedepie (Vasouy)
49.	Le Havre
50.	Bléville
51.	Sainte-Adresse
52.	La Hève headland
53.	Fontaine-la-Mallet
54.	Ecqueville
55.	Saint-Jouin-Bruneval
56.	Fécamp (Val Criquet)
57.	Senneville-sur-Fécamp
58.	Dieppe

1.	Granville (Le Roc)
2.	Guernsey (Channel Islands)
3.	Sortosville-en-Beaumont
4.	Vauville
5.	Beaumont-Hague
6.	Auderville
7.	Gréville-Hague
8.	Landemer
9.	Urville-Nacqueville
10.	Sainte-Croix-Hague
11.	Querqueville
12.	Équeurdreville (Les Couplets)
13.	Cherbourg (Le Roule)
14.	Tollevast
15.	Sottevast
16.	Tourlaville (Les Caplains)
17.	Fermanville
18.	Carneville
19.	Saint-Pierre-Église

THE ATLANTIC WALL

HITLER'S DIRECTIVES FOR THE CONSTRUCTION OF THE WALL

Construction of the Longues-sur-Mer coastal artillery battery, undertaken by the German Navy, began in the autumn of 1943, whereas construction of the Atlantic Wall had been initiated far earlier.

The decision to build a fortified line on the Western European coastline, from the North Cape to the Spanish border, was made by Hitler on the 14th of December 1941, immediately after the United States entered the conflict. In anticipation of the threat of an Anglo-American landing operation behind the German lines, whilst the best part of the *Wehrmacht* was concentrated on the Eastern Front, Hitler announced his intention to build a fortified line along the Western European coastline. By its mere presence and its potential danger to any assailant, the rampart was intended to discourage the Western Allies from any attempted landing operation. The December 1941 directive (*Weisung*) set the order of priorities to be respected to effectively defend the coast: according to the dictator, the seafront between Antwerp and Le Havre was the most vulnerable, followed by the Atlantic coast, the Brittany and Normandy coasts and, finally, the Dutch and Jutland coast.

The multiplication of British raids on the Norwegian and French coasts, over the winter of 1941-1942, together with the success of the first Soviet counter-offensive, which had forced the German high command to retreat from the Channel coastline, had somewhat disquieted Berlin. Hence, Hitler published a second instruction on the 23rd of March 1942 concerning the protection of the Western European shoreline. Whereas the December directive had been a general text outlining the necessity to defend the European coasts, the March 1942 directive addressed the problem of the organisation of coastal defence and entrusted the immense coastal fortification programme to the Todt Organisation.

Firing command post and command post in a long-range coastal artillery battery (17cm pieces), Amfreville (Manche).

The failed Allied raid on Dieppe in August 1942.

A few days before the Dieppe raid (19th August), and immediately after the Canadian operation, Hitler reconsidered the question of coastal fortification during a series of conferences held in August 1942. Whilst the *Wehrmacht* was at a virtual standstill on the banks of the Volga, the dictator was well aware that a landing operation on the Channel coast would herald a major threat and he estimated that some 15,000 bunkers needed to be built along the coast, armed by 300,000 soldiers to ensure coastal surveillance. Finally, he ordered the Todt Organisation to accelerate building work and to finalise the construction of the fortified line by the 1st of May 1943.

Various types of radar installations along the Atlantic Wall. Certain devices were specialised in long-range airspace surveillance, whilst others were charged with providing the *Flak* (aircraft defence) with precious information.

In the autumn of 1943, Field Marshal Von Rundstedt, Commander-in-Chief in the West, drew an alarming portrait of the *Wehrmacht's* position on the Western front in a report he sent to Hitler. Over and above their insufficient numbers, their lack of training and inadequate armaments, Von Rundstedt insisted on the delays encountered in the execution of the coastal fortification programme. Upon this distress signal, in his final directive concerning the Atlantic Wall on the 3rd of November, Hitler announced a series of measures aimed at reinforcing the defensive capacities of the armed forces guarding

Field Marshal Gerd von Rundstedt (left), supreme commander on the Western Front as from March 1942. He was in charge of overseeing construction of the Atlantic Wall.

the coastline. To prove his conviction that the Western front should no longer be neglected to profit the Eastern Front, the dictator appointed the popular Field Marshal Rommel as inspector of the fortifications and to command the battle against Allied invasion. To lead this mission that was of capital importance for Germany's fate, Hitler appointed Rommel to the post of Commander of Army Group B which reunited the 15th and 7th Army, together comprising more than half a million men.

Field Marshal Rommel, surrounded by troops from the *Wehrmacht*, on the English Channel shores.

Inscription on the wall of the Todt battery on the Gris-Nez headland (Pas-de-Calais), addressing the British Prime Minister, Winston Churchill, 'Whoever is insolent, must suffer, you will now pay for your misdeeds.'

THE WALL, ONE OF THE *REICH'S* PRIZED PROPAGANDA TOOLS

Presented as a formidable and armoured concrete barrage, riddled with guns, the Wall was the subject of vast propaganda, aimed, not only at exerting a reassuring influence on German civilians, but also at intimidating the Anglo-Saxon population. As the subject of a great number of articles, photo reports, newsreels and radio programmes, the Wall, which was Hitler's pride and joy, had also become the destination of Hungarian, Bulgarian, Romanian, Italian, Finish, Turkish, Spanish and even Japanese military missions to the Western front.

Fresco on the wall of the Todt battery on the Gris-Nez headland (Pas-de-Calais), '*Gegen Engeland*' ('Against England'). This extract from a famous military march sung by *Luftwaffe* troops in 1940 is accompanied by a painting vaunting the great power of the *Reich* army.

The Todt Organisation was endowed with a highly active propaganda department which produced a multitude of technical sheets to provide to journalists. Here is an example of an article published in the magazine *L'Illustration* in May 1943, '*The wall is even more extraordinary than we ever imagined. The audacity of its design and the quantity of work engaged in its execution are barely believable. The only comparison to be found in history is the great wall erected to fight the Mongol invasions in the North of China,*

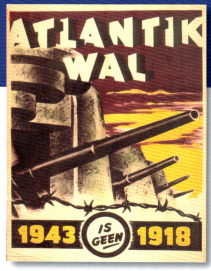

Propaganda poster vaunting the great strength of the Atlantic Wall. On this document drafted in Dutch, the coastal fortification is presented in the form of a continuous and unbreakable line. This extremely concise text claims that 1943 will not be like 1918, the year the Armistice was signed by the Second *Reich*.

along a border of some 3,000km. European coastal protection stretches from the North Cape to the Pyrenean Mountains. Across the 2,700 km of our coastline, there is no spot left unprepared to retaliate against a powerful attack. Immediately after the armistice, the Todt Organisation began fortification of coastal zones along the Channel and the installation of long range batteries firing occasionally towards Dover. It then set to the construction of submarine bases. In February 1942, inspired by experience from the Westwall *(or Siegfried line)* construction, the Führer ordered the edification of the Atlantic rampart. Construction of the former covered an 850km front and included some 22,000 concrete structures.

Anti-tank wall blocking the entrance to a valley.

It had been rapidly built in advantageous peacetime circumstances, whereas the Atlantikwall *was built in the midst of the war, despite enemy airborne attacks and the depletion of efficient means of transport... Six thousand permanent elements and five thousand mobile elements, very high calibre guns fixed onto railway lines and rapid-fire anti-tank guns are all ready for action. Hundreds of thousands of labourers of various nationalities have been employed on this task. Germans provided the teams' framework and represented 10% of the total labour force. As and when the young workers were called to arms, veterans stepped in to replace them. Team leaders commanded from 50 to 200 non-German labourers. The Todt Organisation has in its possession a large number of foreign foremen. Members of the Legion of French Volunteers (LVF) who distinguished themselves on the Eastern Front masterfully managed these teams of French workers, many of whom had already worked on the construction of the Maginot Line. Two hundred thousand Frenchmen, including a number of volunteers have worked on the Atlantic rampart.'*

Of course, the true figures were inferior to those quoted in this article published for propaganda purposes. According to Ob. West (the German supreme command in the Western front) archives, by late 1943, there were, in fact, 2,692 pieces of artillery of a calibre superior to 7.5cm on the Atlantic Wall.

The Sangatte battery

Sangatte was the most powerful coastal artillery battery on the Atlantic Wall. A soldier could literally slip inside this 40.6cm (16 inch) calibre gun to fire across the Channel against the English coast, just thirty kilometres (20 miles) away. Built in 1941, the three casemates that comprised the German artillery position each comprised a huge block of 17,000m3 of reinforced concrete, measuring 50 metres in length and 17 metres in height. The firing chamber was located on the ground floor, whereas the intermediate level housed crew sleeping quarters and the upper level, stocks of water and fuel and electric generators. All the Todt Organisation's propaganda films covered this prestigious battery.

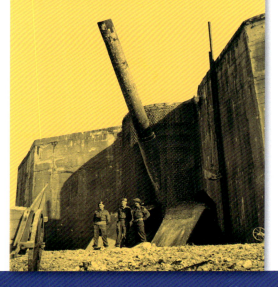

THE TODT ORGANISATION

Created by Hitler and named after the engineer Fritz Todt, the Todt Organisation's main mission was to provide work for Germany's abundant unemployed in 1933. The Todt Organisation's first major project was the construction of German motorways. Then came the construction of what was to be known as the *Westwall* on the *Reich's* Western border. Following France's defeat, the organisation run by Fritz Todt abandoned the Siegfried Line and, within a few weeks, built several major heavy artillery batteries on the Pas-de-Calais coastline, aimed at protecting the fleets that were to land on British soil. The following year, the German construction agency accomplished another great feat by building five submarine bases on the French coast: Brest, Lorient, La Pallice, Saint-Nazaire and Bordeaux.

In the spring of 1942, whilst continuing construction work on the submarine bases and on *Luftwaffe* airfields, the Todt Organisation's major task became the construction of the *Atlantikwalll* on the Western European coastline (Netherlands, Belgium and France). Late 1942, fortification of the French Mediterranean coast was added to the already demanding construction programme.

The Todt Organisation called upon the *Reich's* most influential public works companies to ensure the construction of the fortified line. Unable to guarantee, alone, the completion of the European coastal defence within the given timescale, the German

Construction of a casemate in La Hague, to the west of Cherbourg (Manche).

companies sub-contracted part of the work to certain French public works companies. According to an Allied report based on post-war declarations from ex-executives from the Todt Organisation, in 1944, the German organisation employed between one thousand and one thousand five hundred French companies. Among these entrepreneurs, there were a number of volunteers eager to take part in the Nazi cause and to earn large sums of easy money. It is estimated that they represented approximately a third of the total. Contrary to the companies that voluntarily entered the Todt Organisation, the others were requisitioned and, rather than seeking to satisfy the demands of the enemy, were only looking to protect their equipment and their manpower. Some of these requisitioned companies served the French Resistance, becoming an excellent refuge for STO (Compulsory Work Service) objectors or even as sources of information for the Allies.

Up to the spring of 1942, the Todt Organisation's workforce was relatively mediocre (approximately 70,000 labourers). Facing insufficient volunteers, the occupier exerted pressure on the Vichy government to obtain further manpower. Thanks to an active recruitment campaign, Vichy provided around 200,000 men: French citizens and labourers from the colonies (Africa and Indochina). However, numbers remained insufficient and the Todt Organisation had so-called volunteer workers, as well as forced labourers, brought from occupied Eastern territories (Poland, Czechoslovakia, Russia...). On the eve of the D-Day landings, the Todt Organisation had some 300,000 workers at its disposal in France.

Lines of concrete mixers on a major construction site on the Cotentin peninsula. The Todt Organisation engaged firms with highly efficient equipment.

Tobruk surmounted with an old tank turret, Omaha Beach sector.

ROMMEL AND THE ATLANTIC WALL

Although his reign was brief, Rommel, former chief of the *Afrikakorps*, made a significant impact on the coastal defence system. Contrary to Field Marshal von Rundstedt who, after the war, qualified the wall as a 'monstrous bluff', Rommel had faith in the concrete line's efficacy and did everything in his power to reinforce it.

He ordered the construction of a succession of small concrete forts separated by stretches of uncovered coastline, aimed at forming a continuous defensive cordon, whilst giving a certain depth to the entire blockade. Preferring small construction sites to major installations, which involved lengthy delays and required substantial material supplies and abundant manpower, Rommel multiplied the number of small defensive installations, combat emplacements, trenches, false battery positions aimed at drawing enemy fire, anti-tank ditches and walls as well as concrete nests (or tobruks) housing flame-throwers or surmounted by an old French tank turret.

Rommel (centre), General Marcks, commander of the LXXXIV Army Corps, posted in Saint-Lô (left) and General Speidel, Rommel's Chief of Staff (extreme right).

In the same endeavour to block potential assailants on the beach, Rommel had thousands of obstacles installed along the foreshore. Comprised of wooden or concrete stakes, heavy metallic barriers, tetrahedrons, chevaux-de-frise, hedgehogs assembled with portions of railway track, hundreds of thousands of obstacles aimed at tearing open the

Rommel inspecting the Normandy beaches.

Stakes surmounted with mines and aimed at exploding under the landing barges at high tide.

hulls of landing barges, were arranged in such a manner that they would be effective against any landing attempt, be it by high or by low tide.

As from January 1944, Rommel gave the order to multiply minefields further inland. Although he failed to reach his objective - one mine per square metre of coast - Rommel did, however, have some five millions mines set between January and June 1944. Similarly, he readily opened locks in order to flood the many surrounding marshlands and lowlands, hence protecting over 25,000 hectares from invasion with fresh or sea water. Finally, he ordered for strips of forest to be cut down and for slopes to be cleared of trees in order to plant tens of thousands of wooden stakes across any meadows likely to be used for major airborne operations or for landing gliders. All of this work, feverishly and efficiently executed in the space of only a few months, rendered the Wall an increasingly unbreakable obstacle.

Concurrently, from January to June 1944, the Todt Organisation, in a new lease of life, had managed to erect thousands of small defensive installations bringing the total number of Atlantic Wall elements to around ten thousand. The Todt Organisation's performance was all the more remarkable since, at the same time, it undertook to repair damage caused by Allied bombardments to engineering structures and railway lines as well as the construction of large bunkers aimed at launching secret weapons.

One of Rommel's defence systems for the Normandy beaches: the concrete tetrahedrons can be seen in the background.

The German radionavigation station in Saint-Pierre-Église (Manche) and the Longues-sur-Mer battery in the 1980s:

THE ATLANTIC WALL ON THE EVE OF THE D-DAY LANDINGS

Early 1944, in accordance with Hitler's directive n°51, the Western front was strengthened by a number of human and material reinforcements, whilst Rommel endeavoured to bring continuity and depth to the fortification line. From the autumn of 1943 to the spring of 1944, the number of divisions under the orders of Von Rundstedt increased from thirty-eight to fifty-nine. This figure included ten *Panzerdivisionen* (armoured divisions). With around a thousand tanks, they constituted the striking force that was to throw the Allies back into the sea. Within the German defence strategy, the Wall was only aimed at slowing down Allied progression. Similar progress was achieved on the firing power of the Atlantic Wall fortifications. In June 1944, there were over three thousand pieces of artillery ranging from 7.5cm to 40.6cm, together with thousands of anti-tank guns, machine guns and anti-aircraft artillery. In short, the coastal defence system was far from an illusion. However, as far as the number of guns or the quality of troops was concerned, the Wall was not quite what Goebbels' propaganda would have us believe with his slogan, 'In Dieppe, they held out for six hours, the next time, they won't last an hour.'

'The Shield of Europe'

The caption reads, '*Der schild Europas*' This caricature, published in a *Reich* daily in 1943, perfectly resumes the German defensive strategy along the Western European coastline: the shield (Atlantic Wall) with which Churchill would collide, aimed at slowing down the assailants' progression on the shore - and the two-edged sword (the *Wehrmacht* and its armoured divisions, charged with leading the counter-attack and with throwing the Allies back into the sea).

Coastal surveillance in the Pays de Caux.

their similar configurations are worthy of note.

A THOUSAND BUNKERS FROM THE MONT SAINT-MICHEL TO THE SEINE ESTUARY

The most striking characteristic of the German coastal fortification was its uniformity and its monotony, stemming from the excessive standardisation of its various elements - the only method that could enable the Todt Organisation to guarantee such rapid progress on its construction sites. Mass produced, repetitive, anonymous, devoid of fantasy, damp, unhealthy and designed to kill, the concrete and iron cubes were all alike, as much in terms of materials used, shape, colour, position of openings, entrance defence, construction depth as in terms of interior fittings (armoured doors, ventilation, electricity, telephone, etc.). Among these concrete monsters, today either sand-ridden or overturned on the shore, one can, however, distinguish the ones that were referred to as active (those housing a weapon), the highly varied shelter categories (observation, command, transmission, ammunition holds, garages), underground shelters (workshops, storerooms, depositories, hospitals), as well as special constructions (radar or radionavigation stations and V1 or V2 secret weapon launch bases). Over and above the aforementioned structures, we can add the submarine bases that also included speed boat shelters in Cherbourg and, in particular, in Le Havre.

Open-air artillery battery on circular concrete platforms in the Cherbourg sector (Manche).

In June 1944, from the Mont Saint-Michel to the Seine Estuary, almost one thousand concrete fortifications adorned the 450 kilometres of coastline, along with just as many brick, concrete block or sheet-metal constructions and camps. Despite their great physical resemblance, each and every bunker played a specific role in the coastal defence plan. Since the Germans had no military fleet capable of establishing a sufficiently solid barrier at sea, the long-range artillery batteries, in the form of daunting concrete fortifications built close to the shore, were assigned the task of ensuring the long-distance defence of the *Festung Europa* (Fortress Europe). The numerous smaller constructions housing one piece of low calibre artillery, a machine gun, a grenade launcher or a tank turret, were to ensure close-range coastal defence (against landing barges, tanks or assailants attempting to set foot on French soil).

THE LONGUES-SUR-MER BATTERY

The Longues-sur-Mer battery casemates forming a line.

In June 1944, the Seine Bay (between the Barfleur headland and the Seine estuary) comprised twenty artillery batteries, representing a good hundred guns. Over and above the batteries in Auderville (20.3cm), Amfreville (17cm), Fermanville (Hamburg 24cm), La Pernelle (17cm) and Saint-Marcouf (called Crisbecq by the Americans and armed with four huge 21cm Czech guns), the majority of the Seine Bay artillery positions were equipped with weapons of French origin, with an average calibre of 15.5cm. To the north of Bayeux, just 6 kilometres from Arromanches, more or less in the centre of the profound re-entrant that constitutes the Seine Bay, the Longues battery is one of the most unwonted of the sites that form the landing zone. Built on a treeless plateau, on the summit of a picturesque clifftop, the position comprises four 15cm calibre guns and an observation post located in the foreground, just before the cliff edge. Placed within casemates (bunkers endowed with a large window referred to as a gun port to enable firing), the guns, whose mission was to prevent enemy fleets from approaching the shore, were capable of firing on a target crossing at some twenty kilometres out to sea.

One of the Longues-sur-Mer battery casemates with its gun still in place.

BUILT IN RECORD TIME

Just like all the other major fortified structures that comprised the Atlantic Wall, but with the added curiosity of being situated in the very centre of the future Anglo-American landing zone, the Longues-sur-Mer guns were the target of several aerial reconnaissance missions. For such hazardous investigative missions, the British used high-speed planes, capable of flying at high altitude (30,000 ft), such as Spitfires or Mosquitos, equipped with a narrow-angle lens camera. Thanks to periodical coverage of the coast, the Allied Staff was able to keep up with the Atlantic Wall's advancement. The two following pictures, taken by the Royal Air Force just before the D-Day landings, are an excellent example of the quantity and the accuracy of information offered by aerial reconnaissance, which proved to be the primary source of information to the Allies during the final conflict.

On the aerial photograph dated 2nd March 1944, we can distinguish, in the lower right-hand corner, a few village houses surrounded by planted fields. Between the village and the clifftop that overlooks the Channel, it clearly appears that, three months prior to the launch of Operation *Overlord*, construction of the coastal artillery battery had barely commenced. Three roads had been marked out across the parcels of cultivated land for public works vehicles and lorries. Two major excavation sites, both destined to house a casemate, are perfectly visible on the path running parallel to the coast. Other construction sites, of a smaller scale with the exception of the firing command post on the clifftop, can also be seen on this remarkably clear picture.

Aerial photograph of the Longues-sur-Mer site, dating from 2nd March 1944.

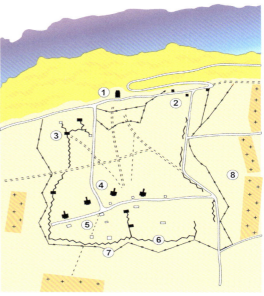

Map of the battery in June 1944

▲ We can easily recognise the four casemates with their guns, the shelters, ammunition holds and, in the foreground, the firing command post. Each artillery position was surrounded by a minefield, the whole forming a strong point.

1. Firing command post – **2.** Tobruk or machine gun emplacement – **3.** Shelter and ammunition hold – **4.** Casemates – **5.** Ammunition holds – **6.** Trenches – **7.** Barbed wire – **8.** Mines

▲ Aerial photograph of the Longues-sur-Mer site, dating from 22nd May 1944.

On the second photograph, taken on the 22nd of May at low tide, the battery construction site had taken on a totally new look. Roads, concrete constructions of all sizes and zigzagging networks of trenches had proliferated. At this point in time, the artillery position resembled a veritable fortress. With a magnifying glass, one can clearly distinguish the four firing casemates deliberately concealed under huge camouflage nets hung on wooden stakes. It would appear that only German companies took part in the construction of the Longues battery, originally a *Kriegsmarine* coastal artillery battery which was retroceded to the German army shortly before the D-day landings. The German firms benefited from manpower comprised of prisoners of war and forced labourers from Eastern Europe. Comparison between the two pictures brings to light the extraordinary efficacy of the Todt Organisation, made possible thanks to excessive standardisation of the concrete elements and the abundant, unrelenting and totally free manpower.

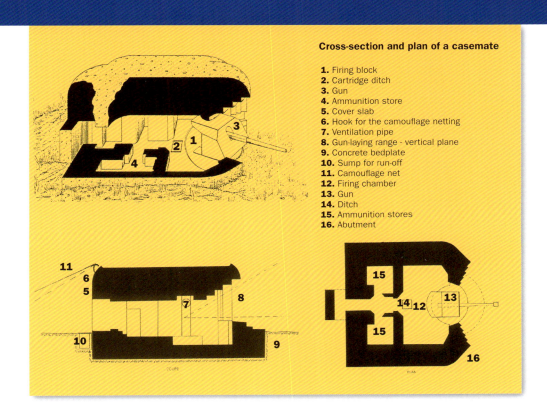

Cross-section and plan of a casemate

1. Firing block
2. Cartridge ditch
3. Gun
4. Ammunition store
5. Cover slab
6. Hook for the camouflage netting
7. Ventilation pipe
8. Gun-laying range - vertical plane
9. Concrete bedplate
10. Sump for run-off
11. Camouflage net
12. Firing chamber
13. Gun
14. Ditch
15. Ammunition stores
16. Abutment

- **The four casemates**

The casemates, huge concrete cubes each housing a piece of artillery, measured approximately fifteen metres in length, ten metres in width for a height of slightly over six metres. The construction of each cube required approximately 600m^3 of concrete and around 4 tonnes of metallic reinforcements. The roofing slab and the walls were just over two metres thick. Such protection rendered the Longues-sur-Mer guns practically invulnerable to aerial bombings.

The casemates were built on a substantial concrete foundation in order to avoid tipping in the case of a projectile exploding close to an abutment. Each casemate consisted of a firing chamber housing the artillery and, to the rear, two smaller chambers for storing ammunition. The trench under the gun was used for storing used cartridge cases. Above the gun, large ducts drew the noxious gases that accumulated in the chamber after a few rounds had been fired.

Sketch of the command post as seen from the sea.

With their large curved contours, the Longues-sur-Mer casemates are partly concealed by a deep layer of earth forming a slope supported on either side of the firing chamber by the abutments. These earthen embankments were also intended to serve as an anti-spalling layer, in other words, they were to absorb the shockwaves of projectiles exploding at the foot of the casemate. The edges of the concrete roof were decked with iron hooks to attach the camouflage netting.

Over two metres thick, the heavy concrete roof slab extended over the gun in a semi-circular visor built in tiers in order to protect the artillery piece against falling projectiles. Facing the sea, each of the Longues-sur-Mer guns had a firing range of approximately 100 degrees horizontally and 40 degrees vertically. The gashes cut into the base of the abutments at either side of the gun were aimed at increasing the firing range by a few degrees to the extreme east and west.

In 1944, several underground shelters were found close to the casemates, serving as accommodation quarters for artillerymen and as ammunition holds. The whole site was protected by machine guns, old tank turrets placed on concrete bases as well as

The firing command post for two casemates in the background.

Command post.

minefields and barbed wire curtains. Hence, each battery formed a genuine small camp entrenched on the edge of the coast.

• **The battery command post**

Located 300m in front of the casemates, on the brink of the cliff, the Longues-sur-Mer battery's half-buried command post comprised two floors. The ground floor housed the observation post with a crenel (frontal gap) largely covering a 180 degree angle, the map room, a telephone exchange and sleeping quarters for gunners.

Under a 70cm thick concrete slab supported by four small steel posts, the upper floor housed the telemetry post (optical device capable of determining the distance of a target). Once the target had been identified by the watchmen, who used binoculars placed on a tripod, and the distance calculated by telemetry, the coordinates were transmitted by telephone to the artillery gunners. One of the most famous scenes of the film *The Longest Day* was shot in the Longues-sur-Mer battery firing command post.

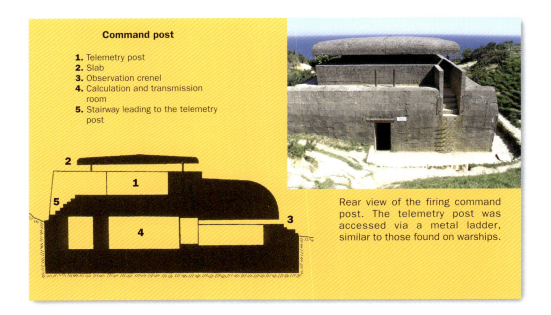

Command post
1. Telemetry post
2. Slab
3. Observation crenel
4. Calculation and transmission room
5. Stairway leading to the telemetry post

Rear view of the firing command post. The telemetry post was accessed via a metal ladder, similar to those found on warships.

Allied bombardments prior to D-Day.

INTENSE ATTACKS BEFORE D-DAY

• **Aerial bombing**

The battery, which was equipped with modern German guns, was located in the very heart of the future landing zone and was capable of firing at approaching assailants on the future British assault position on Gold Beach (Asnelles) and in the American sector on Omaha Beach (Colleville-Saint-Laurent). Hence, to neutralise it, the Allied command decided to conduct aerial bombing on the artillery position over the weeks prior to the D-Day Landings.

The most violent bombing took place between the 28th of May and the 3rd of June 1944. According to a German report, the battery was hit by 1,500 bombs, some of which weighed 2 tonnes and were capable of producing a 7 metre-deep crater. Thanks to their 2 metre-thick ceiling slab and their concrete foundations, the casemates withstood this avalanche of shells, which essentially damaged the transmission lines buried between the command post and the firing blocks. On the night of the 5th to the 6th of June, from midnight to dawn, around 1,200 Royal Air Force heavy bombers set out to drop 6,000 tonnes of explosives on the 10 most incommodious batteries positioned along the future landing zone. At daybreak, 1,400 light and medium bombers from the US Air Force took over and attacked, for the second time in only a few hours, the same 10 batteries. Due to heavy cloud cover, these bombings yielded quite different results from one site to another.

This intense deluge resulted in weakening artillery positions, in producing several hundred craters and in sapping the morale of the German garrisons, who remained barricaded up inside their blockhouses. As an obstacle to the Allied approach on Omaha and Gold, the Longues-sur-Mer battery was a prime target

Allied plane during intense bombardment of German positions.
The Longues-sur-Mer artillery battery's firing range.

Allied bomber flying above the Normandy bocage.

and was consequently bombed by 124 allied planes, unloading 600 tons of bombs, a quantity equivalent to the attack on Pointe du Hoc. Nevertheless, on the morning of the 6th of June 1944, the four guns remained intact.

- **Naval bombardments and German artillery retaliation**

Squadron of A20 bombers from the 9th US Air Force above Pointe du Hoc.

After the aerial attacks, the action plan aimed at neutralising the German coastal guns provided for the naval artillery to enter into action. Hence, a bombardment fleet comprised of thirty four cruisers and battleships and a hundred destroyers took up position, on the morning of the 6th of June, opposite the Normandy shores.

Firing began at daybreak, half an hour before the troops were landed. By then, there was enough daylight for the observers, posted inside the planes that relentlessly circled above the batteries, to guide and adjust the firing coordinates of the huge naval artillery. Here is an extract from the Swedish Colonel B. Stjernfelt's book entitled, *'Alarm i Atlantvallen' (Alarm in the Atlantic Wall)*, on the subject of the Longues-sur-Mer battery, *'The Longues battery was rapidly engaged in combat against the allied naval forces. It opened fire for the first time at 05:37, twenty minutes before sunrise. Ten sprays of water rose from the Channel close to the* US Emmons *destroyer. Furthermore, the battery targeted the battleship* Arkansas *that was busy firing to cover the Omaha sector. No less than 17km separated the battery from its target. The battleship retaliated with twenty 305mm shells* and one hundred and ten 127mm shells. The battery then ceased fire and pointed its guns eastward. Closer targets had come into its firing range. Landing in the British sectors was taking form and the command ship Bulolo, the flagship transporting the entire staff of the Gold Beach assault troops, had just anchored at approximately 12,000m from the coast facing Longues. At 05:57, the battery opened fire on its new target which was covered with huge bursts of seawater and was obliged to withdraw seawards before being hit... The cruiser

Coastal surveillance radar after RAF machine gunning.

Ajax *immediately came to the rescue. After an artillery duel at a distance of 11,000 metres, during which the cruiser fired one hundred and fourteen 150mm shells, the Longues battery temporarily ceased firing at 06:20. When the landing operation began on Omaha Beach, the battery resumed fire, showering the troops on the shoreline. Against Gold Beach, the battery entered rapidly into action and its gunfire was, apparently, efficient. However, because of the limited firing range of the concrete-covered artillery pieces, only those situated on the wings were able to precisely target the narrow*

A *Würzburg* radar after Allied aerial bombing. This detection apparatus was used to guide *Flak* fighter planes.

Allied warship off the Normandy coast on the morning of 6th June 1944.

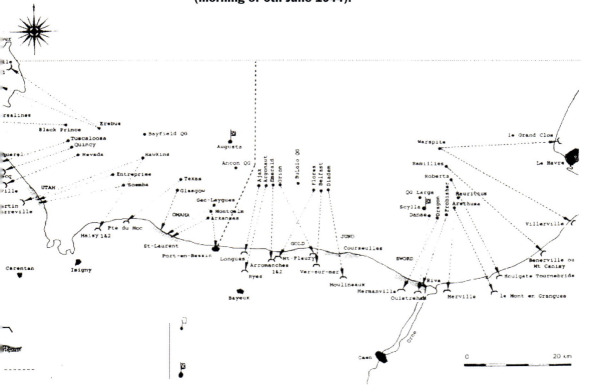

Neutralisation plan for the German coastal artillery batteries (morning of 6th June 1944).

strip of beach. Twice more, the Allies opened heavy artillery fire on the battery. Since the objective was to reduce the battery's artillery to silence as quickly as possible in order to avoid them causing disastrous losses among troops and material, the cruiser *Argonaut* came to assist the *Ajax*. When both ships had fired thirty-six 150mm and twenty-nine 130mm shells, the battery finally ceased fire. It was 08:45.'

Gunfire from the warships had caused considerable material damage. Of the four artillery pieces, three had been put out of combat. Thanks to radar, the British cruiser *Ajax* had fired with exceptional accuracy, thus accomplishing an unquestionable feat of strength. The Swedish Colonel, a specialist in German artillery on the Atlantic Wall, added, *'This is only the British version of the combat between the Longues battery and the Allied naval* forces. It is extremely incomplete. In the same sector, the French cruisers *Georges Leygues* and *Montcalm* were attached to the Omaha Beach support sector, and were operating with the American battleship *Arkansas*. *The Georges Leygues was the first to open fire at 05:37 with a 152mm shell (and not the Ajax as claimed by the official British report), soon to be followed by the* Arkansas, *which suffered a close shave, after which the two French cruisers continued firing. The German fire ceased after retaliation from the* Montcalm. *The battery resumed fire in the afternoon and it was only then that the Ajax, which belonged to the Gold sector support forces, entered into action. The French cruisers were engaged in combat against the battery shortly after 17:00 when the Ajax signalled to them with a projector to cease fire against the Longues battery which was now her affair! The Georges Leygues, however, continued firing and pulled off two strikes on the fortification shortly before 19:00. As soon as it was possible to examine the debris on site, fragments carrying the unquestionable signature of French projectiles were found among the shrapnel.'*

USS Arkansas opened fire on the morning of the 6th of June 1944.

The Saint-Marcouf-Crisbecq (Manche) artillery battery

This position, which was equipped with 20.3cm Skoda guns, suffered intense bombing prior to the 6th of June. In contrast with the Longues battery, the Saint-Marcouf garrison withstood the American attack over several days before retreating to the fortress of Cherbourg.

THE SURRENDER OF THE LONGUES GARRISON

On the morning of the 7th of June, the Devonshire Regiment's Second Battalion, a unit belonging to the 50th Northumbrian Division's 231st Infantry Brigade, which had landed on Gold Beach the previous day, approached the battery from the east. With its 200 gunners of an average age of 40 to 45 years, the Longues-sur-Mer garrison surrendered to the British troops without resistance, contrary to those defending the Saint-Marcouf battery, located behind Utah Beach, who withstood the American assault until the 11th of June. Once more, according to Colonel Stjernfelt, the Longue-sur-Mer battery gunners' morale was at an all time low. They reckoned that captivity was the most secure and the fastest way to put an end to the war, hoping to be sent to America as prisoners.

Gold Beach (Asnelles) on the morning of the 6th of June. The landing barges are visible, as is the unloading of heavy vehicles. It was a British unit, landed on Gold Beach, that captured the Longues battery on the morning of the 7th of June.

• **The Atlantic Wall, a futile fortification?**

Despite the immense scale of construction work, executed in record time on the European coastline, the German defence system's resistance to the attacks it suffered in Normandy in June 1944 was a major disappointment. In spite of this defeat, the defence of the Western European coastline did play a significant role in German operations and in the advancement of the conflict in general. The support offered by the fortification during the final confrontation with the Anglo-Americans was well below the German command's expectations. The reasons for this are to be found equally in the system's failings as in the strategy implemented by the Allies.

General Eisenhower in Normandy.

Far from complete and far from resembling a wall; in other words a continuous obstacle approximating a concrete barrage, the Atlantic Wall was in fact a more or less regular succession of solidly fortified elements corresponding to major ports between which there were extensive and insufficiently secured gaps. This vast ongoing construction

The Atlantic Wall was to be perceived as a continuous line across the entire Atlantic and Channel coast.

Casemate and two-level firing command post at the German artillery position in Vasouy, the twin sister to Longues.

site - the coastal fortification - one of the very bases of the *Reich's* defensive strategy in the West, was, in 1944, no more than a linear system, lacking in depth and whose value was unbalanced from one location to another. Without wishing to neglect the danger it represented to assailants, the Wall was, first and foremost, a symbol of prestige and intimidation.

The defeat of the fortification was also largely due to the Allied assault strategy. Judging that the shortest route to invade Germany from England was in the Pas-de-Calais region, and never - or at least too belatedly - having imagined that the Allies would attempt a landing operation without entering major ports, the German command had quite logically concentrated its major defence positions between Dunkirk and Le Havre and had articulated its entire system around major ports, which they believed to be inevitable itineraries for the assailant. By carrying out their amphibian attack between major ports, on exposed beaches and what's more, to the south rather than to the north of the Seine, the Allies were to brilliantly bypass a system that had not been designed to face such an eventuality. The uniquely original character of the landings on the 6th of June needed to throw the German command off balance and paralyse its reflexes. Despite its weaknesses and its defeat during its first confrontation (the Wall was overcome before midday on the 6th of June on four beaches and, by evening on Omaha

Dawn – 6th June 1944 – landing operations on Gold Beach (Asnelles), the British landing zone.

Beach) the fortification was not for as much totally unprofitable to the *Reich*. The Atlantic Wall had, above all, obliged the Allies to give up any plans to land in the Pas-de-Calais region, where the German defensive organisation was at its strongest, hence abandoning highly superior strategic potential towards the Ruhr. The coastal defence also obliged the Allies to undertake substantial preparatory manoeuvres and to gather considerable resources which would not have been necessary had the coast been totally exposed. In short, the Atlantic Wall represented a considerable hindrance to the general advancement of the conflict.

The incredible deployment of Allied forces on Omaha Beach.

Montgomery (left) and Leigh-Mallory, Air Commander-in-Chief for operation *Overlord*.

- **The Longues-sur-Mer battery after the German retreat**

After the surrender of the German troops defending the Longues-sur-Mer battery, Royal Air Force engineers took control of the clifftop and set up an airfield, known as B 11 and which was operational from the 26th of June to the 4th of September. Equipped with a 1,200m landing strip covered with a square-linked metal grid, this airfield was designed to accommodate fifty aircraft. According to certain witness reports, the airfield was behind the destruction of the fourth casemate to the east of the battery. In order to protect the B 11 installations, the British are said to have installed a DCA (anti-aircraft defence) post on the roof of the bunker and to have stored, inside the casemate, ammunition that exploded for some unknown reason. It was the violence of this explosion that caused the destruction of the concrete cube together with its gun, and not, as can often be read, a shot from Allied naval artillery.

▲ Panoramic view from the firing command post. The casemates can be seen on the left.

Panoramic view to the west, towards the American sector on Omaha Beach and Pointe du Hoc.

The casemates are approximately seventy metres apart.

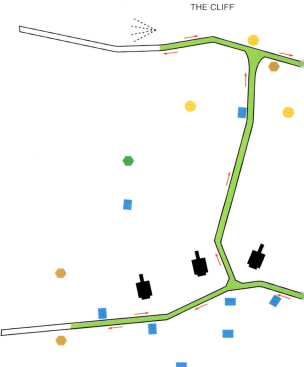

THE CLIFF

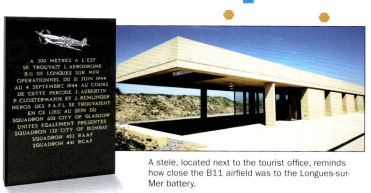

A stele, located next to the tourist office, reminds how close the B11 airfield was to the Longues-sur-Mer battery.